STUCK IN A LIFT FOR 3 DAYS: THE MUSICAL

SCRIPT & LYRICS

by

ROBIN CALVERT

Approx Duration: 2 hours

www.robincalvert.co.uk

https://www.facebook.com/robin.calvert

Twitter: @ROBIN_CALVERT

As a result of cost-cutting greed, an ambitious City property developer finds time on her hands over the course of one weekend…

Written March-April 2017.

ACT 1

CURTAIN RISE

1. INT. BOARDROOM. DAY.

VICTORIA KING (29, tall, cool, professional, ruthless. Blonde lacquered hair scraped back over a high forehead. Smart sharp business suit, necklace, rings and high heels, she swings in with her entourage:-

Secretary HELENA, a poorer woman's version of her ten years older. PA STEVE (steadfast young man, circa 25, with open filofax). And lifestyle coach MR. FLORES (balding man with a committed but dazed look, in open-necked shirt wearing New Age symbols).

The SHAREHOLDERS wait patiently around a large conference table, portfolios, reports and figures at the ready. Mostly EXECUTIVES, pinstriped or otherwise, usually suited, but what look like one or two members of the public, relations, in comfortable slacks and coats.

A large plaque together with a framed recent photo of Victoria (same hairstyle) receiving an award reads "TOP PROPERTY DEVELOPER OF THE YEAR".

All the while Victoria is singing "I'M AT THE TOP OF MY GAME" (upbeat, high activity):

> VICTORIA:
> (singing)
> (VERSE) *When I'm in first gear and my performance can't be faulted*
> *When I'm top at results my drive can't be halted*
> *People say I'm crazy, but they're just jealous*
> *But it's a long climb to the top and you don't wanna stare down*
> *You just gotta maintain your position on the ladder*
> *You just gotta sustain your condition with your bladder -*
> *(whispers) haemorrhoids, but women never admit to them, unless they have to*
> *It took such a long time to get here, or there (whatever tense were talking in)*
> *What's mine is mine is mine, so butt off*
> *You couldn't step in my shoes and travel as far*
> *They wouldn't fit you, so please*
> *(whispers f-off)*

Victoria & Entourage take up positions. Victoria at the head of the table, though looking out over a panorama of London that includes the LondonEye and the Shard. Helena beside her. Steve and Mr. Flores take a back seat at opposite sides of the table behind the Shareholders, but nearby.

> VICTORIA & ENTOURAGE:
> (CHORUS) *I'm At The Top Of My Game and I'am the Dealer*
> *I'm the Go-To Person for definitive oddities*
> *My reputation precedes as a first-class spieler*
> *I'm the No 1 seller in certain commodities*
> *My name is known throughout the City*
> *Stencilled in gold leaf on my mahogany door*
> *But as for me-time... (sighs) that's a pity*

Victoria moves away from the window to place both hands either side of her black plastic swivel chair nearby.

> VICTORIA:
> (VERSE) *When momentum's on my side, all things considered*
> *When I walk that walk, contract's sealed and delivered*
> *People say I'm power-mad, but wouldn't they like it*
> *It's a long climb to the top and you don't wanna stare down*
> *You just gotta maintain your position on the ladder*
> *You just gotta sustain your condition with your bladder*
> *It took such a long time to get here, or there, (whatever tense were talking in)*
> *What's mine is mine is mine, so butt off*
> *You couldn't step in my shoes and travel as far*
> *They wouldn't fit you, so please*
> *(whispers f-off)*

> VICTORIA & ENTOURAGE:
> (CHORUS) *I'm At The Top Of My Game and I'am the Dealer*
> *I'm the Go-To Person for definitive oddities*
> *My reputation precedes as a first-class spieler*
> *I'm the No 1 seller in certain commodities*
> *My name is known throughout the City*
> *Stencilled in gold leaf on my mahogany door*
> *But as for me-time... (sighs) that's a pity*

REPEAT CHORUS

Victoria makes a decisive hand gesture. Music stops.

> VICTORIA:
> Helena, Steve, Mr. Flores. Shareholders.

She remains standing.

> VICTORIA:
> Here at Victoria King Enterprises, we don't
> promise the quickest time from property development start-
> up to completion for fun. We also guarantee the biggest
> profits.

Victoria reaches for a remote and activates a projector screen to the right of the
blinds, high on the wall (above Steve).

First, a slide of a new business block.

> VICTORIA:
> Fennell Square. Celebrating its fifth anniversary. Centrally
> located, designed by Mackie, owned by us. Sold to a
> Chinese conglomerate for 1.75 billion.

Next: a holiday complex abroad, surrounding a lake.

> VICTORIA:
> Manygates Lake, Zurich. Up two years. Has helped the
> regeneration of tourism in the area. We have our eyes on
> another property nearby, which could be linked.

Next: The tallest building of the three, close to the Thames. "THAMES
TOWER" seen emblazoned across the front.

Before Victoria can start about this the oldest shareholder, pinstriped
CHAMBERS, 65, raises a hand, as if expecting permission to speak.

> CHAMBERS:
> I wonder if sometimes we aren't too quick. (opens a file)
> The 2015 report on subsidence at the Neville Falls Memorial
> Park- (cut off)

VICTORIA:
(cutting in) Neville Falls insisted on having its own surveyors on the payroll.

CHAMBERS:
Thereby cutting our own liabilities.

VICTORIA:
That was the way *they* wanted. In any case, there was limited evidence of subsidence.

CHAMBERS:
(waves file about) Enough for this.

VICTORIA:
That came from a resident.

CHALMERS:
Well it would be a resident, wouldn't it? (looks around) Since they can see it.

VICTORIA:
A resident who went to the papers who in turn approached the rival bidders for the site. That report was seriously skewed.

CHALMERS:
And as it turned out, the foundations.

He taps headlines on Page 3 of THE TIMES. "NEVILLE FALLS AGAIN". A gaping hole appears beneath a water wheel adventure ride.

VICTORIA:
If there was a lesson, it is from now on, we survey ourselves.

CHALMERS:
That's a discreet way of admitting the report was right. (shrugs to the other Shareholders) Isn't it?

VICTORIA:
If the opposition had taken Neville Falls on,

there'd still be hard hats on the ground.

CHALMERS:
Better hard hats than subsidence.

Before Victoria can retort:

CHALMERS:
There is, I think, a case against cheaper
subcontracts and increased profit margins, which
only risk safety.

VICTORIA:
(thumps table) I'am proud to deliver the biggest
wage and bonuses in the City.

A smart tough-looking man in a crewcut and dark-blue suit, 32, BRAYNE,
politely intervenes.

BRAYNE:
There is so much good news to share to our
shareholders. (gestures) It's not all doom and
gloom.

Brayne casts a withering look Chalmers way. He requests to take the
newspaper from Chalmers, who relents. Brayne then turns it to another page:
"THAMES TOWER OPENS NEXT WEEK".

BRAYNE:
Thames Tower. Our most ambitious project yet.

VICTORIA:
My magnum opus.

BRAYNE:
A staggering 250feet in height, it's the tallest residential
block in London.

Brayne looks directly at Victoria.

BRAYNE:
Who's to say… that one day, when your career is

done, they won't erect a statue in honour of you. As they did your namesake…Victoria.

Victoria quite taken aback by Brayne's flattery – and he knows it.

> STEVE:
> You need to report on Thames Tower for social media before noon.

> HELENA:
> (opens her diary) Before your one o'clock appointment with Lardel.

> VICTORIA:
> So I do.

> MR. FLORES:
> Just do what you can. What you need to do.

Helena & Steve regard Mr. Flores as an alien from another planet.

A good-looking softer-faced man, WALTER, 26, appears concerned by the mutual lingering eye-contact between Victoria and Brayne.

She becomes aware Walter is looking at her and breaks it off with Brayne.

> VICTORIA:
> Well, if there's anything else…it can wait.

As she makes to leave, Walter makes to block her.

> WALTER:
> I must talk with you urgently.

> VICTORIA:
> You have far from a monopoly on my time.

> WALTER:
> (whispers) That's what I want to talk about.

Exit Victoria and Walter.

Brayne takes command of the boardroom meeting.

> BRAYNE:
> Let's get to the next item on the agenda, shall we?

Helena gets up to lower venetian blinds on sunlight coming through the windows. She then approaches front of stage and LOWERS VENETIAN BLIND DRAPES.

THE DRAPES WITHDRAW, PULLING THE BOARDROOM SET BACK.

WHEN THE VENETIAN BLINDS ARE REOPENED BEATS LATER, WE'RE IN:

2. EXT. PARK. DAY.

Leafy, twisty turning, with various pleasant features including a mini-maze, a bench and a water fountain shaped like a peacock with water protruding through the wings of the birds. Sunlight and blue sky above. Walter sings the way he feels ("A DETOUR IN THE PARK" – pleasant, romantic).

> WALTER:
> (singing)
> (VERSE) *Let me show you a place off the mainstream*
> *Away from the hurly-burly of life*
> *It's just off the main road, turn left at the crossroads and*
> *turn left again.*
> *This is my park, so pleasant and green*
> *Secluded and serene.*
> *I can lose myself in it's warm grace*
> *This can be your park, so friendly and springlike*
> *Private and snug*
> *You can lose yourself in its tender embrace.*
>
> (CHORUS) *Let me take you for a Detour In The Park*
> *See what a difference it makes*
> *All man-made problems put in perspective*
> *Put your hand in mine and trust the Fates*
> *We were once children, bright and blessed at birth*
> *There's another way if only we can find it*
> *Where Mother Nature comes down to earth*

So, let me take you for a Detour In The Park
See what a difference it makes.
(double echo) A Detour In The Park
See what a difference it makes
(angelic echo) A Detour In The Park

VICTORIA:
(singing)
(VERSE) *I belong and work in the mainsteam*
In the centre of the hurly-burly of life
Turn right, right again at the crossroads and onto the main road
That is my Park, so busy and hectic
Crouded and competitive
Mind diverted in all comings and goings
This is me: adrenalin and caffeine
Power and possession
Losing myself in its controlling intensity

WALTER:
(CHORUS) *Let me take you for a Detour In The Park*
See what a difference it makes
All man-made problems put in perspective
Put your hand in mine and trust in the Fates
We were once children, bright and blessed at birth
There's another way if only we can find it
Where Mother Nature comes down to earth
So, let me take you for a Detour In The Park
See what a difference it makes.
(double echo) A Detour In The Park
See what a difference it makes
(angelic echo) A Detour In The Park

(MIDDLE-8) *I want to find a girl just like you*
To be with at work and then at night
A relationship that satisfies all the boxes
To love and cherish with all my might.

VICTORIA:
(MIDDLE-8) *I could fall in love with you, my dear Walter*
But then where would I be?
My freedom gone, independence deserted

I'm thinking of my power you see.

WALTER:
(still singing) *Won't you take this Detour with me?*

VICTORIA:
(still singing) *We already have. A Detour is not forever.*

WALTER:
Will you?

She puts finger to his lips.

VICTORIA:
(softly) *And neither will I.*

Music fades.

VICTORIA:
But I thrive on life. They are my meat, my drink. They provide the grist to my mill. Without them, I wouldn't have been made Top Property Developer of the Year.

WALTER:
You told me I don't have a monopoly on your time. Well, neither do you on Brayne.

VICTORIA:
What are you driving at?

Walter hesitates.

VICTORIA:
Come on. You've come this far. Spit it out.

WALTER:
He has a girlfriend who works in stocks and bonds.

Victoria frowns at Walter, sizing him and the information up.

VICTORIA:
Had.

WALTER:
He's still seeing her.

Victoria looks angry.

VICTORIA:
And how would you know?

Before Walter can provide further information, Victoria holds up a hand and gestures tersely.

VICTORIA:
Nice try. But me and Brayne are not actually together…
(pause before) Yet.

Walter shrugs hopelessly.

VICTORIA:
Maybe I don't want the kind of relationship you need. I worry about stifling my freedom, my independence, my power.

WALTER:
(holds arms out either side) What? With me?

VICTORIA:
And I do like to be in control.

WALTER:
And you choose him over him.

VICTORIA:
I've had one debate this morning, Walter. I won't countenance another. Goodbye.

She breaks away. Then feels guilty, adding:

VICTORIA:
Of course, it goes without saying I expect you to be in the office Monday morning.

WALTER:
What for?

VICTORIA:
To work! (checks watch) I'm late already.

Victoria makes to exit.

WALTER:
(pointing after her) Where are you going?

She's gone.

WALTER:
(singing glum, with half-hearted musical accompaniment)
(CHORUS) *Let me take you for a Detour In The Park*
See what a difference it makes
All man-made problems put in perspective
Put your hand in mine and trust in the Fates
We were once children, bright and blessed at birth
There's another way if only we can find it
Where Mother Nature comes down to earth
So, let me take you for a Detour In The Park
See what a difference it makes.
(sighs, talking) I guess I'll have to take this Detour
again…Alone….

As Walter walks back the way he came stage left, the trees move with him – eventually supplanted for a clear view of

EXT. THAMES TOWER.

Victoria produces a large set of keys that jangle.

VICTORIA:
(to herself) One look from Thames Tower before it opens to the public on Monday.

She throws the keys up in the air, catches them and walks past a tree out of sight.

CURTAIN.

3. INT. LIFT, THAMES TOWER.

STAGE CENTRE VISIBLE ONLY, with floor walls either side & black drapes either side of that.

The lift is gleaming metallic, with coloured lights at the top which refract off the polished surface.

Door opens. Victoria steps inside.

She presses for the top-floor. The indicator rises from 1 on its way through a maximum of 70.

Victoria looks up impatiently.

>VICTORIA:
>Come on.

The indicator reaches the top-floor of 70 and she lets herself out.

Victoria exits the lift into the **CORRIDOR (STAGE RIGHT)**.

Using the keys she lets herself into one of the **SUITES (EXTREME STAGE RIGHT)**.

New-age décor. Smart, unlived in. Victoria lets herself in, producing a bottle of champagne and a glass from her expensive designer bag.

She pours and takes a look across at the London skyline.

>VICTORIA:
>(singing)
>(VERSE) *When I'm in first gear and my performance can't be faulted*
>*When I'm top at results my drive can't be halted*
>*People say I'm crazy, but they're just jealous*
>*But it's a long climb to the top and you don't wanna stare down*
>*You just gotta maintain your position on the ladder*
>*You just gotta sustain your condition with your bladder –*
>*(whispers) haemorrhoids, but women never admit to them,*

unless they have to
It took such a long time to get here, or there (whatever tense
were talking in)
What's mine is mine is mine, so butt off
You couldn't step in my shoes and travel as far
They wouldn't fit you, so please
(whispers f-off)

Victoria raises a glass. Back-projection zooms in on the Queen Victoria statue.

> VICTORIA:
> (CHORUS)
> *I'm At The Top Of My Game and I'am the Dealer*
> *I'm the Go-To Person for definitive oddities*
> *My reputation precedes as a first-class spieler*
> *I'm the No 1 seller in certain commodities*
> *My name is known throughout the City*

Victoria burps and steadies herself.

> VICTORIA:
> (half-singing)*Stencilled in gold leaf on my mahogany door.*

Victoria toasts the view.

> All my own work.

Victoria toasts the suite around her.

> VICTORIA:
> All my own doing.

She takes one last look out and around before leaving.

Victoria exits the suite, locks the door and presses for the lift.

Several beats pass and nothing happens.

She is just to head through a door marked "STAIRS" when the lift arrives with a high-pitched squeal.

The doors slide ominously open. Victoria steps inside.

She stabs at the lift controls. The door clanks shut.

Black drapes block off left and right of the lift, while we expand on the lift a little.

Victoria presses for the ground floor.

On its way past 50 the indicator begins to slow down. Victoria gestures it on agitatedly.

It comes to a dead halt at 40.

Lift doors open. Open black drapes before Victoria pops her head out. Another door marked "STAIRS".

She shuts the lift doors and presses "GROUND" again. Close black drapes.

As the lift resumes its downward movement, Victoria impatiently gestures for the indicator to get there.

It comes to a slowdown at 35 and stops completely at 30.

Victoria leans back as the lift hydraulics stop. She presses "EXIT". Nothing happens.

Victoria presses again – twice.

> VICTORIA:
> Come on, come on, you stupid thing.

Still nothing.

> VICTORIA:
> Calm down. Give it a few seconds.

She counts to ten. Then presses Exit again. Nothing.

Victoria waits another ten seconds, then presses again.

And, without waiting, again.

VICTORIA:
Come. On. You stupid thing!

She twists and jabs the buttons desperately, until one or two of the lights behind them go out.

Victoria gasps. The indicator and controls are lifeless.

VICTORIA:
(singing) How come I press for the ground floor, but end up on the 30th?

Victoria looks from the lift as if disappointed it didn't give her an answer. She opens her mouth and hands wide.

VICTORIA:
(singing "THAT FRANTIC FEELING")
(VERSE) *There's no life in the doors however I press*
I'am utterly trapped in here today
Worse time of them all for a power cut
How unlucky, for once, you say:
No one ensures CCTV is manned
No one rushes to rescue the damned
I'm in the grip. Of...

CHORUS:
That Frantic Feeling
Oh what it is to be on your own
That Frantic Feeling
Oh suddenly I can't bear to be alone.
That Frantic Feeling races through your brain, paralysing your thoughts,
Deadening your heart, killing your soul
That...Frantic...Feeling!

VERSE:
There's no caretaker booked until Monday
I'am utterly alone til then
Worse still, in a box 10 by 8
My mistake – but then:

Victoria tries to phone Brayne.

VICTORIA:

Brayne. Come on.

She shakes her head as she cannot get a signal.

> VICTORIA:
> (MIDDLE-8) *No one answers the phone when you ring*
> *No one hears the screams that can bring*
> *The grip. Of...*
>
> CHORUS:
> *That Frantic Feeling*
> *Oh what it is to be on your own*
> *That Frantic Feeling*
> *Oh suddenly I can't bear to be alone.*
> *That Frantic Feeling races through your brain, paralysing*
> *your thoughts,*
> *Deadening your heart, killing your soul*
> *That...Frantic...Feeling!*

She looks at the phone, shakes and throws it to one side. Clattering to the floor beside her.

> VICTORIA:
> (screams the song title "CLAUSTROPHENIA")
> Suggest weird acoustics on this track.
> (VERSE) *Claustrophenia!*
> *I'm feeling Claustrophenia*
> *More than simple hysteria*
> *It's such a confining feeling I'm in*
> *Feeling less than Claustrophenia*
> *Swallowed up in its vice-like grip*
> *Unable even to take the dip*
> *Claustrophenia!*

One woman barber shop quartet where Victoria repeats the title "CLAUSTROPHENIA" repetitively in alternating cadents and sequence.

> VICTORIA:
> (VERSE) *My whole mind and body is embalmed in*
> *Claustrophenia*
> *More than simple hysteria*
>
> *It's such a confining feeling I'm in*

Feeling less than Claustrophenia
Swallowed up in its vice-like grip
Unable even to take the dip
Claustrophenia!

REPEAT CHORUS.

At the end of which Victoria faints.

CURTAIN FALLS.

END OF ACT 1.

ACT 2.

CURTAIN RISE.

LIFT, THAMES TOWER – CENTRE STAGE.

OPEN BLACK DRAPES STAGE LEFT, REVEALING:

4. INT. SUITE, GRAND HOTEL.

Imperial pillars. Key colours of cream, gold and black.

Brayne is overseeing arrangements by liaising laptops with an attractive event planner, YVONNE: late 20s, built-up hair and thin glasses in a tight-fitting dress.

With him is a very aristocratic lady, an older version of Victoria in her early 60s. This is ELIZABETH, Victoria's mother. And a man who despite his formidable lined face has twinkly eyes and a sense of humour, PATRICK, also in his 60s.

> BRAYNE:
> Caterers – check. DJ – check.
>
> ELIZABETH:
> Victoria.
>
> BRAYNE:
> Check.
>
> ELIZABETH:
> But where is she?
>
> BRAYNE:
> She's not supposed to know about all this, Elizabeth.
>
> ELIZABETH:
> My daughter is the only person I know who arranges her own surprise birthday parties. You know as well as I she set this up.

BRAYNE:
She put her trust in me to deliver. Believe me, she's busy enough.

Elizabeth turns to Patrick.

ELIZABETH:
Patrick. I still feel we should have heard from her.

PATRICK:
Don't forget, she's the opening of Thames Tower on Monday.

ELIZABETH:
(sighs) I worry that one day my daughter will crash and burn.

Patrick puts his arm around Elizabeth.

PATRICK:
I'm very proud of what Victoria is achieving.

ELIZABETH:
(hint of irony) Aren't we all?

Patrick links arms with Elizabeth and together with Brayne they exit.

The Caterers & other helpers continue getting the suite ready for the birthday party WHILE:

INT. LIFT, THAMES TOWER.

Victoria wakes up, initially panicked.

VICTORIA:
(VERSE) *Around me, they contain me.*
Taunt me, intimidate and scare me.
Moving closer, surrounding, enveloping.
Encircling, enforcing, entwining.
Tighter, closer, tighter, pressing, holding, containing,
forcing, imposing, strangling.
The life out of me.

(CHORUS) *Oh God*
The Walls Are Closing In On Themselves
And now
I'm diminished to the size of elves
Oh God
The Walls Are Closing In On Themselves
But for
The fact I'm wearing high-heeled boots
I would
Be poured down the nearest chute

(VERSE) *Against me, they flatten me*
Roll, straighten and pulverise me
Moving closer, suppressing, suffocating
Omnipresent, oppressive, o-pon me
Flatter, colder, harder, heavier, uncaring, unfeeling,
inhuman, murdering, killing
The life out of me.

(CHORUS) *Oh God*
The Walls Are Closing In On Themselves
And now
I'm diminished to the size of elves
Oh God
The Walls Are Closing In On Themselves
But for
The fact I'm wearing high-heeled boots
I would
Be poured down the nearest chute

(MIDDLE-8) *And no one will know this moment until it's*
too late
And no one can help me from this Fate

(CHORUS) *Oh God*
The Walls Are Closing In On Themselves
And now
I'm diminished to the size of elves
Oh God
The Walls Are Closing In On Themselves
But for
The fact I'm wearing high-heeled boots

I would
Be poured down the nearest chute

(MIDDLE-8 REPRISE) *And no one will know this moment*
until it's too late
And no one can help me from this Fate

(CHORUS) *Oh God*
The Walls Are Closing In On Themselves!

(not singing) I'll send a text to Walter.

BLACK DRAPES STAGE RIGHT REVEALS:

INT. WALTER'S PAD.

Comfortable bachelor apartment with nice curtains and sofa. Walter reaches for
a bottle of vodka and starts to pour a very large measure.

BLACK DRAPES BLOT HIM FROM VIEW.

In the lift Victoria picks up the phone, remembering…

Still on her knees, she starts banging on three of the walls. It goes on for at least
half a minute.

She then looks cynically at her hands and slowly brings them to rest.

> VICTORIA:
> Just calm down. Pretend you're about to go into the
> boardroom. (smiles) Yeah. That makes you feel so
> confident, so good. (leans back) But before you get that
> way, what do you do?

LOWER A BLACK DRAPE SHOWING A PROJECTED IMAGE of
Victoria meditating in a pink balloon.

Victoria repeats the same posture, hands upturned on her knees and closes her
eyes. As she begins, raise the image out of sight.

She gets lost in meditation for several beats. Then begins deep breathing.

VICTORIA:
It will only be a matter of time before help comes.
Someone's got to check up on the Tower. It opens on
Monday.

(singing "CAN'T SOMEONE HELP ME")
(VERSE) *It isn't my fault I was in the wrong place at the*
wrong time
It isn't my fault I chose this particular day
I'm not psychic, watching out for a sign
I was just unlucky I hope I hear you say

(CHORUS) *I'm sitting here all frightened and alone*
I'm sitting here with no signal on my phone
Can't Someone Help Me
Why won't someone come
Why not the sound of footsteps
Can't Someone Help Me
Why can't something be done
Why can't I hear your voice
Can't Someone Help Me
Today

(MIDDLE-8) *How much longer must I stare at these four*
walls
How much longer before cramp sets in
I should have paid for back-up I recall
The sniffer dogs won't now begin

(CHORUS) *I'm sitting here all frightened and alone*
I'm sitting here with no signal on my phone
Can't Someone Help Me
Why won't someone come
Why not the sound of footsteps
Can't Someone Help Me
Why can't something be done
Why can't I hear your voice
Can't Someone Help Me
Today

REPEAT CHORUS

Victoria sighs and looks around the lift, as if expecting something to change.
She's getting pretty fed up, closes her eyes and when she opens them again, it's
the same metallic walls looking at her.

> VICTORIA:
> (singing to a different melody) *If I never see that colour
> again...*

She turns round and looks up.

> VICTORIA:
> Maybe I should look at the lights.

She wears a silly smile on her face and after several beats almost drops off.

> VICTORIA:
> Or come up with another song. Nothing about what I'm
> actually going through at the moment either. Too
> depressing.
>
> (singing "CAMOLA, THE NONSENSE SONG").
> (VERSE) *Camola was a girl I knew from my way way back*
> *Camola was my best friend of all time*
> *Camola is the be-all and end-all of this tale*
> *Because I just made her up for this rhyme.*
>
> *Camola is as good a name as any*
> *Yet I can't say I've heard it before*
> *It just sprang to my memory banks when I was searching*
> *And next thing, she's the stuff of folklore*
>
> (CHORUS) *I'm bored out of my tree*
> *And something had to be invented for me*
> *To while away the hours in this lift*
> *Is too heavy going a shift*
> *Hence, Camola (The Nonsense Song)*
> *Nonsense to anyone but me.*
> *Camola (The Nonsense Song)*
> *Really makes perfect sense, you see.*
>
> (VERSE) *Camola was the brightest, best and most likely to*
> *With three husbands she surely did*

One of them was my first crush
And our friendship as we knew it was got rid
Camola was out of the strata
Camola was a byword for pain
Camola was persona non grata
Camola was never mentioned again

(CHORUS) *I'm bored out of my tree*
And something had to be invented for me
To while away the hours in this lift
Is too heavy going a shift
Hence, Camola (The Nonsense Song)
Nonsense to anyone but me.
Camola (The Nonsense Song)
Really makes perfect sense, you see.

At the end of it Victoria laughs out loud.

> VICTORIA:
> Jeez. That was scary. That I could make perfect sense of saying the first thing that came out of my mouth. Pity I can't do the same with my mind.

She gestures impatiently to her temple.

> VICTORIA:
> I just need to switch off in here! (pause) You know what it is, don't you, Victoria? You've got no-one else to give orders to.

Victoria looks up, a smile fading.

> VICTORIA:
> The lift is unresponsive and the phone useless. You're on your own. Ssh. Be quiet!

Victoria listens out for something. There's nothing.

> VICTORIA:
> There you go. Total silence. (swallows) How boring. You may as well be dead. (thinks again) Or asleep.

She changes position as if to avoid cramp.

> VICTORIA:
> But you're not tired yet. Or should I say, I'm not tired yet.
> (hands to head) Ah. You're doing it again. (releases head)
> You're doing all this to yourself.

Pause.

> VICTORIA:
> (seriously) We're doing it to each other.

Another pause.

> VICTORIA:
> There is no 'we'. Only me. And, as I told Walter, that's just
> the way I like it.

Mournful violin music plays around Victoria.

Victoria looks around, trying to determine whether it's coming from inside or
outside the lift.

> VICTORIA:
> (to the lift) Can you please turn that off? I hate that
> stuff.

The music continues to play.

> VICTORIA:
> God. Is that how bad I feel about Walter?

The music stops on a discordant note.

> VICTORIA:
> Yep. It is. OK. Switch off the chatterbox. (pause,
> before) Come to think of it, that's another song.
>
> (singing "SWITCH OFF THE CHATTERBOX").
> (CHORUS) *Why didn't Walter listen*
> *Can't remember where I was going*
> *Or did he take his dismissal to heart*

And am I reaping what I was sowing

Did I correct the latest figures
Adjusted to a degree
Or did they just scoop them up
And took them as Gospel to a tee

My mind skips from subject to subject
Like a social butterfly
Some chance of being social in a solitary lift
But in my mind I jump with a sigh.

(CHORUS) Switch Off the Chatterbox
Just Switch Off The Chatterbox
Before your system overloads and you can't take anymore
Switch Off The Chatterbox
Just Switch Off The Chatterbox
Before your brain explodes on these four walls and your
heart...sinks to the floor

(VERSE) Why won't Brayne call out the dogs
Am I so forgettable
What or who is he thinking of
I shall make his actions regrettable.

Should I have dismissed Chalmers
The end of his opinions and (gestures) sever
He's been part of the furniture
Been on the board forever

My mind skips from subject to subject
Like a social butterfly
Some chance of being social in a solitary lift
But in my mind I jump with a sigh.

(CHORUS) Switch Off the Chatterbox
Just Switch Off The Chatterbox
Before your system overloads and you can't take anymore
Switch Off The Chatterbox
Just Switch Off The Chatterbox
Before your brain explodes on these four walls and your
heart...sinks to the floor

She settles down for the night.

OPEN BLACK DRAPES ON THE RIGHT REVEALING:

INT. LOUNGE, PARENTS' HOME.

Expensively furnished. Elizabeth is pacing up/down, her hand around a low hung necklace, while Patrick pours brandies at the bar.

> ELIZABETH:
> I'm concerned about Victoria.

> PATRICK:
> Well I wish you wouldn't be. Victoria can take care of herself. (soda in brandy) Top Property Developer Of The Year, for goodness sake. Or have you forgotten?

Elizabeth gives up the necklace, stops pacing and takes her brandy, sitting down. Patrick retires to his comfy armchair and unrolls the FT.

> ELIZABETH:
> Patrick, there is something wrong.

Patrick lifts the paper up, points to the front page "GOLD SHARES IN TURMOIL" and taps it.

> PATRICK:
> You're telling me!

> ELIZABETH:
> But that's just it, don't you see? Victoria always telephones you Friday evenings to tell you her end of week figures.

> PATRICK:
> (considers, before) She has missed before. Like when she has a new man, for example. After all, I don't insist upon it. And she's certainly no daddies girl.

He's almost rebutting an accusation.

PATRICK:
And with the party Saturday. Thames Tower on Monday.
I'm sure she hasn't given it a thought.

Patrick lifts the paper back up to read.

PATRICK:
Neither should you.

REPLACE THE DRAPES ON THE RIGHT.

Clock moves to 1.00am, by which time Victoria is sleeping.

Moves onto 3.00am, when Victoria wakes, as if from a bad dream of suffocation. She realises it's true and feeling stifled.

VICTORIA:
(sings bars of *"Claustrophenia"* & *"The Walls Are Closing In On Themselves"*.
(talking singing) *Wait. Stop. Remember.*
Deep breaths. (deep breathing) *Keep control...*

Victoria adjusts to her new reality wearily and slumps back down to sleep.

Clock continues on its way to six o'clock. Cue musical symbol of a dawn chorus. She sleeps through that so the clock continues on to eight o'clock.

Victoria stirs and catches sight of it. She comes to eagerly, leaning upright. Reaching out, in vain. She looks up at the lift walls.

VICTORIA:
You don't do coffee, do you? (thinks again) Not even on my birthday. (gestures the wall away) Doesn't matter. Any minute now the janitor will come and I'll be out of here with a double expresso, to celebrate in style.

The lift fails to answer back.

VICTORIA:
What's that? (pauses before, getting louder) I don't even hear you.

Something hits her.

> VICTORIA:
> (quoting herself) "There will be no need for a janitor until seven o'clock on the day Thames Tower opens, on Monday". (curses) Stupid bitch. No janitor, no security guard. Why did I ever say that?

She bows her head.

> VICTORIA:
> To cut more corners. (sighs) Well, some corner I've cut for myself here right now.

Her arms flop to either side.

> VICTORIA:
> Better wait for the inspection team on Monday then. Although if they're expecting me to be out there…. (pause)

She's utterly fed up and slumps back to sleep.

Clock continues all the way through to noon, then stops as Victoria awakens, relatively refreshed and surprised to find herself that way.

> VICTORIA:
> (singing "I'LL THINK OF DAFFODILS IN SPRING")
> (VERSE) *It's a lovely sunny Spring day, outside these four walls*
> *And I can't see one ray of sun*
> *The only gleam comes in silver*
> *And that's too dull a gold for fun*
> *At such a time as this, thoughts turn to romance*
> *But my heart's as heavy as lead*
> *Blocked off from springing*
> *I may as well be dead*
>
> (CHORUS) *I'll Think of Daffodils In The Spring*
> *Even if I can't see them*
> *I'll Think of Daffodils In The Spring*
> *Even if I can barely imagine them*
> *I'll pretend to be a Daffodil In Spring*

Just to escape the present day
I'll embrace the role and blow in a wind

Until I no longer feel that way
I'll Think of Daffodils, like some wartime weepie
I'll Think of Spring, like some parkhouse keeper
I'll Think of Daffodils in Spring

(VERSE) *The sap is rising, beyond these metal confines*
But I can't see one bud in bloom
The only relief is stark
And that's too sad to give room
At such a time as this, the pace quickens in the City
But I'm out of the loop by a mile
I may as well be overseas
For I cannot see your smile

CHORUS:
I'll Think of Daffodils In The Spring
Even if I can't see them
I'll Think of Daffodils In The Spring
Even if I can barely imagine them
I'll pretend to be a Daffodil In Spring
Just to escape the present day
I'll embrace the role and blow in a wind
Until I no longer feel that way
I'll Think of Daffodils, like some wartime weepie
I'll Think of Spring, like some parkhouse keeper
I'll Think of Daffodils in Spring

Victoria sits back, happy. But it doesn't last.

VICTORIA:
I'm going to miss my own party and be in no state for the unveiling on Monday morning. How dumb is that?!

As Victoria reflects bitterly, we **DRAW BLACK DRAPES ON THE LEFT REVEALING:**

INT. SUITE, GRAND HOTEL.

As yesterday, only with more STEWARDS. Brayne answers his phone, listens a few beats, before.

> BRAYNE:
> Well I haven't seen her. (bites lip) I wasn't expecting too. (pause) I doubt she's gone off with Walter, Elisabeth. She told me she was going to dump him. (listens a beat) Because the relationship wasn't going anywhere. (pause) Yes. (Another pause) Well, she did tell me. So I doubt she'll be with him.

Brayne removes the handset away from his ear while the caller gets irate.

> BRAYNE:
> Elizabeth. Walter is no serial killer. But I will phone around. Look at it this way, everyone's going to be here tonight. And that includes Victoria.

DRAW BLACK DRAPES TO.

INT. LIFT, THAMES TOWER.

Victoria, sprawled against the lift door, sings "I WISH I WERE IN LAS VEGAS 1974".

> VICTORIA:
> (VERSE) *I wish I could score jackpot on this machine*
> *One chance pull and the metal no longer looks mean*
> *Cascading down my freedom clean*
> *The most glistening sight I have ever seen*

As the song gets underway, the **BLACK DRAPES OPEN STAGE REVEALING:**

INT. 1974 CASINO NIGHTCLUB

CUSTOMERS in check or flared safari suits, with perms, sideburns &/or moustaches, playing roulette (CROUPIER, FLOOR STAFF) or dining before a CABARET SINGER.

If it weren't for the fact he's wearing a black rather than white sequinned jumpsuit, he could be taken for Elvis. Though his hair is blond and he has a prominent Zapata moustache and dimpled chin. Lights proclaim him to be "WAYNE DENT".

> VICTORIA / WAYNE DENT:
> (CHORUS) *I Wish I Was In Las Vegas 1974*
> *To feel the way I saw in a movie once before*
> *The white jumpsuit, sequins, quiff I so adore*
> *Climbing onto the stage with Elvis*
> *Around the floor…*

And Wayne Dent is singing the song with Victoria from the lift, despite the fact they're in two different time zones and locations. Occasionally leading the lyrics, urging her to finish.

> VICTORIA/WAYNE DENT:
> (VERSE) *Moustache, musak and magic was the name of the day*
> *It was better than this ol' lift that's blocking my way*
> *Rose-tinted glasses keep bad memories at bay*
> *And nostalgia stops the mind from depressive decay*
>
> (CHORUS) *I Wish I Was In Las Vegas 1974*
> *To feel the way I saw in a movie once before*
> *The white jumpsuit, sequins, quiff I so adore*
> *Climbing onto the stage with Elvis*
> *Around the floor…*

As things progress, Victoria closes her eyes.

A VICTORIA LOOKALIKE - younger, more carefree, not the absolute ruthless professional - is handpicked by Wayne Dent to join her on stage.

> WAYNE DENT / VICTORIA LOOKALIKE:
> (VERSE) *I wish I were at the casino tables on a date*
> *To throw a dice and risk it all on an eight*
> *To climb right into a sportscar, feel my fate*
> *Climbing out barefoot only to unlock the gate*

REPEAT CHORUS

Victoria in the lift sighs longingly at song's end as Wayne Dent embraces the Victoria Lookalike. Much applause.

Wayne Dent may be Walter in subconscious disguise. Walter playing two parts.

VICTORIA:
I used to be nice like that. Reputation doesn't go
hand in hand with niceness. (looks around) I won't even
be missed.

**AS WE CLOSE THE BLACK DRAPES ON THE LEFT (LAS VEGAS),
OPEN ON THE RIGHT REVEALING:**

INT. SUITE, GRAND HOTEL.

The GUESTS including Elisabeth, Patrick, Helena, Steve & Mr. Flores, start to
arrive. Brayne much in evidence, being the perfect host. We don't hear any
actual words.

Meanwhile, the clock on the lift wall escalates to evening. Past six, past seven,
to eight o'clock.

Elizabeth looks around at the still-arriving guests.

ELIZABETH:
There's no sign of Walter.

BRAYNE:
And we're not likely to, if Victoria has ended the
relationship, are we?

STEVE:
She never ran it past me.

MR. FLORES:
So long as she ran it back her inner psyche, I don't care what
she confided in me…or otherwise.

A thought strikes Patrick.

PATRICK:
My God. She hasn't fired him from the board, has she?

HELENA:
Why would she?

> PATRICK:
> I was about to say. We need his expertise.

Elizabeth looks at her watch.

> ELIZABETH:
> It is now eight o'clock.

> HELENA:
> Any minute now…

Elisabeth nudges Patrick in the direction of the TOASTMASTER, a pompous-looking man in red uniform polishing his glasses before a speech.

> PATRICK:
> Almost my dear. She always did like to make a grand entrance. After everyone else.

> ELIZABETH:
> Assuming she's not lying dead in a ditch somewhere. Oh, I wish I'd sent a text.

The clock reads 8.15. Waiting Staff ready to encircle, the Toastmaster getting impatient to deliver, while Guests openly mutter about Victoria's non-attendance. Now even Brayne begins to look troubled.

> ELIZABETH:
> (to Patrick, aloud) What do you hope to gain from this constant prevaricating? We are merely making sure she isn't!

She produces her phone.

> ELIZABETH:
> Police!

The Guests gasp.

> PATRICK:
> (to himself) Come on, Victoria! Where on earth are you?

CURTAIN FALLS:

INTERVAL:

CURTAIN RISE:

5. INT. LIFT, THAMES TOWER. EVENING.

VICTORIA, now getting used - if not quite resigned - to her predicament. At this juncture she sings as much to pass the time as express her anxieties and emotions.

TO THE LEFT OF VICTORIA IN THE LIFT, we see news spread throughout the Guests in **SUITE, GRAND HOTEL.**

Brayne steps forward, whispering in the Toastmaster's ear. He starts to quibble, but is reassured. He throws his napkin down in disappointment and rips the speech up.

> VICTORIA:
> (singing "HE'S HAVING FUN WITHOUT ME")
> (VERSE) *I can just sense what he's about*
> *Even though I just can't get out*
> *I can just feel: I don't matter*
> *Out of sight, out of mind*
> *Out of mind, he'll so unwind*
> *Into the lap of the first girl to pout*
>
> (CHORUS) *He's Having Fun Without Me*
> *Without Me*
> *Without Me*
> *He's having his cake*
> *Indulging his tricks*
> *Living it up, getting his kicks*
> *He's Having Fun Without Me*
>
> (VERSE) *I can just imagine where he's at*
> *Now I can only worry*
> *I can just visualise: I'm out of his world*
> *Not seen, nor heard*
> *Or heard... (chuckles in spite of herself). So absurd*
> *He's forgotten I exist and won't do sorry*
>
> (CHORUS) *He's Having Fun Without Me*
> *Without Me*
> *Without Me*

He's having his cake
Indulging his tricks
Living it up, getting his kicks

The air-conditioning makes a funny noise.

Victoria looks sharply up to it, but it resolves itself.

SUITE, GRAND HOTEL.

Brayne addresses the Guests.

> BRAYNE:
> There will be a simple explanation for Victoria's no-show…

> ELIZABETH:
> Yes, that she needed our help a lot sooner than we gave it.

> BRAYNE:
> But, as a precaution and… (gestures to Elizabeth) as you just heard, the police are being called.

> PATRICK:
> Of course, she could just be stuck in traffic. If she does show now, we're all going to have egg on our face.

Elizabeth turns to face Patrick.

> ELIZABETH:
> I sincerely hope we are.

In the centre of the stage - the **LIFT** - the air conditioning starts making the faulty noise intermittently.

Victoria gets to her feet and jumps up to get a purchase on the vent.

Her long fingernails prove a hindrance and she starts to snap several off.

One goes badly and she starts to bleed.

> VICTORIA:

Oh damn it.

She gets out a handkerchief, but the bleeding continues. The air conditioning

sounds seriously off-beam. She looks up desperately.

>VICTORIA:
>Oh no!

Victoria starts to panic, but tightly binds the finger with the handkerchief.
Waiting on tenderhooks during:

SUITE, GRAND HOTEL.

As the Guests start to disperse, Brayne receives a text on his phone.

>BRAYNE:
>Hang on, hang on. The police request everyone remain.
>They just want to find out as much as possible.

Some Guests prepared to argue for their right to leave, until Elizabeth steps
forward.

>ELIZABETH:
>If we could all pool our knowledge of Victoria's last-

She stops herself.

>ELIZABETH:
>Of her movements… (fighting back tears) I would be most
>grateful.

Patrick moves in close to console her. The Guests – some of whom call others
back in - relent.

They chatter among themselves DURING:

LIFT, THAMES TOWER.

Victoria removes the cloth around her finger. It has stopped bleeding.

She sighs in relief and makes for the vent again.

After an incredibly laborious procedure, during which Victoria grunts, groans and screams to resounding effect, she manages to unscrew one side of the vent – then the other.

She slides her other (non-bloodied) hand in – and hastily retracts it.

>VICTORIA:
>Ouch.

Before sliding it in again.

Using her handkerchief to clear a large ball of fluff, the air conditioning starts to behave normally again.

Leaving the vent off, Victoria sinks to her knees.

>VICTORIA:
>Thank God for that. (pause before) And you know you won't have to wait until Monday. People are bound to sound the alarm when you don't show up to the party.
>(singing)
>
>(VERSE) *It's the last hour you'll feel this way*
>*It's just about to happen*
>*The end of purgatory*
>*When feet begin a-tappin'*
>
>(CHORUS) *Any Minute Soon*
>*They will arrive*
>*Any Minute Soon*
>*It will be over*
>*Any Minute Soon*
>*I will survive*
>*Any Minute Soon*
>*I'll be in clover*
>
>(VERSE) *It's the last moment I'll be like this*
>*It's just about to begin*
>*Bye bye, blessed torment*
>*My mouth opens to sing*
>(CHORUS) *Any Minute Soon*
>*They will arrive*
>*Any Minute Soon*
>*It will be over*
>*Any Minute Soon*

I will survive
Any Minute Soon

I'll be in clover

REPEAT CHORUS

Victoria stares hopefully into the future.

SUITE, GRAND HOTEL.

POLICE INSPECTOR WHITING arrives. On the young side, with styled
blonde hair, a direct gaze and a square jaw, he looks a determined customer.
Instead of a notepad, he produces his phone on voice record.

> INSP WHITING:
> Police Inspector Whiting.

> ELIZABETH:
> Thank God you've arrived. We're all very worried about the
> disappearance of my daughter. The property developer
> Victoria King?

Insp Whiting isn't overly impressed.

> INSP WHITING:
> I'll need to take statements from everyone. But I'll start
> with you. When was the last time you spoke to your
> daughter… Ms King?

> ELIZABETH:
> (singing) *I had to think twice, it was such a non-event.*
> *Just one of those exchanges one takes for granted. Even*
> *though it could be…*(sniffles) *the last time.*

> PATRICK:
> I'm sure it won't be.

> ELIZABETH:
> (still singing) *I wish I could be as sure as you.*

> INSP WHITING:

(singing himself) *And when did you last speak to her?*

ELIZABETH:
(singing) *I prefer 'previously spoke together'.*

INSP WHITING:
(makes a note, not singing) *Previous.*

ELIZABETH:
(singing) *Last Wednesday. At eight o'clock. I was just about to get the mints out, when she rang.*

INSP WHITING:
(singing, turns to Patrick) *Was that the last time you spoke to her, sir?*

PATRICK:
(singing) *No I-* (cut off)

INSP WHITING:
(singing until otherwise noted) *And you are?*

ELIZABETH:
(singing) *This is my husband, Inspector.*

PATRICK:
(singing) *And Victoria's father. I'm a stockbroker, she's a property developer. We talk shop over brunch.*

ELIZABETH:
(sighing while singing) *Such a lot of shop.*

INSP WHITING:
(singing) *Did she look...* (gestures to Patrick) *...or sound...* (gestures to Elizabeth) *strange?*

ELIZABETH/PATRICK:
(in unison) *Perfectly normal and* (with same melody) *"Top Of Her Game".*

Brayne steps forward.

BRAYNE:

(not singing) She worked the same magic in the boardroom the day she went missing.

INSP WHITING:
(singing) *And you are?*

BRAYNE:
Brayne. I'm on the board and consider myself a close friend.

ELIZABETH:
(singing) *Close?*

BRAYNE:
(singing momentarily) *Closer than Walter.* (Pause before) *Now.*

PATRICK:
(singing) *I see…*

ELIZABETH:
(no longer singing) Inspector. This is her birthday party. Why isn't she here? Three Days before she opens Thames Tower?

INSP WHITING:
(singing) *In view of the date and the upcoming event on Monday, Victoria's disappearance is a cause for concern.* (pause before) *We need to alert the media.*

Patrick looks apprehensive.

ELIZABETH:
(singing) *It has to be done. If we are ever to find her again.*

Patrick nods reluctantly.

They all look up as a large TV screen on the wall above comes on.

TV NEWSREADER:
(singing) *Victoria. Victoria. Victoria King. Is Missing. Not presumed dead. That would be too ghastly to*

contemplate. Ask her mother.

ELIZABETH:
(singing, to audience) *Yes. Just ask me!*

TV NEWSREADER:
(singing) *So full of life and (melody) on Top of Her Game…
Victoria King, 28, was voted Top Property Developer of the
Year. Her reputation precedes her. Only next week she was
due to unveil Thames Tower, the second tallest building in
London, second only to the Shard.*

PATRICK:
(interjects singing) *With plans to build the tallest.*

TV NEWSREADER:
(singing) *Duly noted. With plans to build the tallest.*
(peering out to address all viewers) *Where is she? And on
her birthday? All her family and friends await her, tonight
in vain. We must find her. If you know where she is, please
get in touch and we will treat any information in the strictest
confidence.* (pause before) *Not on your Nellie.*

TV Newsreader giggles adolescently, before a free hand pours a glass of water
over his head.

ELIZABETH/PATRICK/DET-INSP WHITING:
(in unison at the TV screen) *So long as you confide in us!*

CURTAIN FALLS STAGE LEFT:

LIFT, THAMES TOWER.

VICTORIA:
(singing "WHY WON'T SOMEONE COME?")
(VERSE) *How much longer before they remember who
I'am
How much time must elapse before I can
See the light of day again
Step into sunshine, when?
How long is it to be?*

(CHORUS) *Why Won't Someone Come?*
I mean, Why Won't Someone Come?
Are they sulking, determined to punish
Are they happy, holding their airbrush
Why Won't Someone Come?
Today

(VERSE) *How much longer before they drop the amnesia*
How much stronger to ward off a seizure?
That might kill me off at my prime
Write me out permanently, flatline
How long is it to be?

(CHORUS) *Why Won't Someone Come?*
I mean, Why Won't Someone Come?
Are they sulking, determined to punish
Are they happy, holding their airbrush
Why Won't Someone Come?
Today...

Victoria tails off, deflated.

VICTORIA:
No one knows I went back to Thames Tower on Friday. No
one...except Walter...and he's probably put me out of his
mind by now. (sighs) So...here's to my second night in the
lift. The second of three it seems.

Victoria tries to get to sleep, but restlessly tosses and turns.

VICTORIA:
(singing "WHAT DO I CARE?").
(VERSE) *What's the point in hoping*
This nightmare will end soon
It will just go on and on and on
Making its point, spreading my doom
Time for me to leave the room
(looks at the lift ironically)
Up here, all right?

(CHORUS) *What Do I Care?*
If this is where I end up
Tough shit, as they say

What Do I Care?
If no one gets to me in time

I'd bite the bullet now, if I could
What Do I Care?

(VERSE) *What's the point in dreaming*
Any second you will wake
When you are already awake, awake, awake
This is it, for goodness sake
Time has left it too late
Time for me to leave the room
(looks at the lift ironically)
Up here, all right?

(CHORUS) *What Do I Care?*
If this is where I end up
Tough shit, as they say
What Do I Care?
If no one gets to me in time
I'd bite the bullet now, if I could
What Do I Care?

CURTAIN FALLS CENTRE STAGE:

CURTAIN RISES STAGE RIGHT:

6. INT. POLICE INTERROGATION ROOM.

Walter before Inspector Whiting. Recording apparatus switched on by a Female Constable also present. Singing until otherwise stated.

>WALTER:
>We were together in the boardroom. Then we went for a
>(sings melody) *"Detour in the Park"*.
>
>INSP WHITING:
>On a workday?
>
>WALTER:
>I had something important to tell her.

INSP WHITING:
What?

WALTER:
It was private.

INSP WHITING:
(singing) *You are being interviewed under caution.*

WALTER:
I asked her to marry me. She said no.

INSP WHITING:
(singing) *You are being interviewed under caution.*

WALTER:
But I accepted it. Why would I want to get my revenge?

INSP WHITING:
(singing) *You are being interviewed under caution.*

WALTER:
I'm not that kind of man. And I will do anything to help find her.

INSP WHITING:
(singing) *You are being interviewed under caution.*

WALTER:
(angrily singing) *I'am innocent!*

Insp Whiting leans forward, a smirk on his square jaw.

INSP WHITING:
(no longer singing) Until proven guilty.

CURTAIN FALLS STAGE RIGHT.

CURTAIN RISES STAGE CENTRE:

7. INT. LIFT, THAMES TOWER.

Victoria taking stock.

VICTORIA:
(to herself & the audience) The last few years have been one mad rollercoaster. I mean, they've put me where I'am. But... (singing) it's only when you're on your own you've got the chance to take stock.

(singing "IT DOESN'T REALLY MATTER IF TIME TICKS").

VICTORIA:
(VERSE) *There's a clock on the wall of this lift*
And it ticks
Counting down to my destruction is all
There's a clock on the wall and it scares me to death
Bearing me down
While it stands tall

(CHORUS) *It doesn't really matter if time ticks*
You can't stop it, so what's with all the hysterics?
It will just go on
With or without you along
You may as well get used to the sound of ticking now
It doesn't really matter if time tocks
You can't halt it, so what's with all the mental blocks
It will just go on
With or without you along
You may as well get used to the sound of tick-tocking now

(VERSE) *There's a clock on the wall of this lift*
And it tocks
Louder and louder it gets all the time
There's a clock on the wall and it fills my head
Giving me migraines
While I want to play dead

(CHORUS) *It doesn't really matter if time ticks*
You can't stop it, so what's with all the hysterics?
It will just go on
With or without you along
You may as well get used to the sound of ticking now
It doesn't really matter if time tocks
You can't halt it, so what's with all the mental blocks
It will just go on

With or without you along

You may as well get used to the sound of tick-tocking now
(now talking) In fact, I've started to relish time to think
things out.

Victoria pretends she has her own personal audience (us).

VICTORIA:
Here's another one for you. In keeping with my present
state of mind, which is a work in progress. See what you
think.
(singing "SAVED MYSELF FROM BURN OUT").
(VERSE) *Maybe I've made mistakes*
Cut corners in my haste to the top
Profit a must, I made money the gist
Quality compromised, safety at risk
Why else would I be stuck in this lift?
Why else should I be the one on the late shift?

(CHORUS) *But maybe I've Saved Myself From Burn Out*
Snatched away from that merry-go-round
Saved Myself From Burn Out
Against my wishes, I'm unbound
Free to take stock
Before I end up in the dock
And labelled the architect of my own downfall
So take a deep breath and use this time
Alter your course, make your life rhyme
And Save Yourself From Burn Out

Save Yourself From Burn Out

(VERSE) *Maybe I've made mistakes*
Wanting it all not today but yesterday
My ego around me, I carried a mirror
Profit a must, I made money the gist
In the big league and trending on Twitter
In the fast lane for the gold to be fitter

(CHORUS) *But maybe I've Saved Myself From Burn Out*
Snatched away from that merry-go-round
Saved Myself From Burn Out

Against my wishes, I'm unbound

Free to take stock
Before I end up in the dock
And labelled the architect of my own downfall
So take a deep breath and use this time
Alter your course, make your life rhyme
And Save Yourself From Burn Out
Save Yourself From Burn Out

(and talking singing) *And at least I can get engrossed in my thoughts with no outside distraction.*

Victoria subsides to touch base again.

CURTAIN RISES ON THE LEFT, REVEALING:

INT. PARENTS' HOME. EVENING.

Darkness for a few beats, then sounds of Elizabeth and Patrick approaching. Light comes on in the lounge, with Elizabeth's hand on the light-switch.

> ELIZABETH:
> I'm shocked on more than one level. I'm shocked Victoria's jilted Walter for Brayne.

> PATRICK:
> Leave that to me. He's been dating a heiress for three years and, only last month, engagement was on the cards.

Patrick makes for the bar.

> PATRICK:
> It's time someone put Victoria straight.

> ELIZABETH:
> Maybe she already knows. And doesn't care.

> PATRICK:
> Brayne has a reputation for being a womaniser. He's utterly ruthless, works his way through women on his way to the top.

ELIZABETH:
Maybe that's what our darling daughter finds so appealing.

PATRICK:
She wouldn't want to be discarded. And that's what he does.

ELIZABETH:
Not everyone can be so rational in matters of the heart as you can the outlook of a cash forecast, Patrick dear.

Patrick hands her the drink.

ELIZABETH:
So why didn't you steer her straight?

Patrick looks at her – as if that would have helped.

They sit and talk quietly DURING:

INT. LIFT, THAMES TOWER.

Victoria looks more reflective.

VICTORIA:
So I'm stuck here because I cut corners. (singing) Not just one, but many. Cost effective, staff reductive, micro management.

(singing "ONE THING AT A TIME").

VICTORIA:
(VERSE) *Split our mind in two, then four and then eight*
Develop the mental limbs of an octopus
Multi-tasking can show the way
Do everything at once and accomplish

But I'm not a machine
I'm a flesh and blood woman
Stuck in a machine that's broken down like my soul
Stuck in a chasm overlooking a deep hole
A metaphor for a breakdown, so I'm told

(CHORUS) *From now on*
One Thing At A Time
Don't try to reinvent the wheel
Remember, take it as a sign
To keep things on an even keel
You burn so brightly, you'll burn to your heels
You'll end up doing less in the fall-out
From now on
One Thing At A Time
(One Thing, Just One Thing,
But One Thing, Just)
One Thing At A Time.

(VERSE) *Multiply your to-do list, filofax and diary*
Pretend you're the latest computer instore
Multi-tasking can teach you the way
To take the brakes off so you feel the core

But you're only a human being
Not a perfect download
Stuck in a machine that's broken down like my soul
Stuck in a chasm overlooking a deep hole
A metaphor for a breakdown, so I'm told

(CHORUS) *From now on*
One Thing At A Time
Don't try to reinvent the wheel
Remember, take it as a sign

To keep things on an even keel
You burn so brightly, you'll burn to your heels
(fingers warns us) *You'll end up doing less in the fall-out*
From now on
One Thing At A Time
(One Thing, Just One Thing,
But One Thing, Just)
One Thing At A Time.

Victoria leans back.

VICTORIA:
You know, I'm almost sad this will be my third and last

night.

There is an abrupt noise that should have the audience reeling in their seats. It is an exaggerated version of the noise used to denote the air conditioning earlier.

> VICTORIA:
> Oh my God. I might yet pay the ultimate price!

She checks her watch and looks up at the clock on the lift wall. Midnight.

STAGE LEFT Elisabeth and Patrick exit for the bedroom.

Victoria takes her heel off, but the noise just as abruptly abates.

> VICTORIA:
> Eight hours to go.

Rather than put the heel back on, Victoria settles down to sleep. Lights dim.

Clock on the lift wall goes from midnight. Victoria asleep until three…

when the clock stops and the air conditioning starts up again.

Victoria grabs her shoe and forces the heel into the air conditioning vent. The noise abates to some extent.

She settles down. Resume fast forward motion of the clock, with Victoria

finally nodding off at 4.00.

The noise returns at 5.00, but she ignores it and by 6.00am wakes, feeling stifled.

Victoria sets to with the shoe. It takes longer this time.

> VICTORIA:
> Oh well. That should give me a couple more hours of oxygen, surely. Won't be too bad if I can last an hour before they come and rescue me.
>
> (sings bars of *"Save Myself From Burn Out"* & *"One Thing*

At A Time").

If the Tower opens at nine, the janitor and security must come by seven. Surely? (pause as she struggles to

remember) Oh, what did I say?

Dawn rises on the City.

Victoria, now inhaling at six o'clock, has another go at the air conditioning vent. This time the noise remains.

She urges clock to move forwards to seven o'clock.

Slowing down but far from real time, the time progresses to five past, ten past, quarter past. All the while Victoria waits and gasps...in vain.

Now finding it difficult to breath – and with the air-conditioning louder than it's ever been - Victoria slumps to one side, half-fighting, half-resigned.

The clock grudgingly moves towards 7.20.

CURTAINS PART ON THE LEFT:

INT. FOYER, THAMES TOWER.

Enter the JANITOR, who sets to with mop, etc.

Young uniformed SECURITY GUARDS log in. Security Guard 1 makes for the lift, realises it is jammed.

Almost as if she can see them, Victoria calls out:

> VICTORIA:
> (shouting) I'm up here!

Security Guard 1 takes the stairs and, next beat, **APPEARS:**

INT. CORRIDOR, THAMES TOWER.

Security Guard 1 is about to climb up the stairs to the next floor when he hears Victoria's muffled shouting and banging. **(MEANWHILE, CURTAINS CLOSE EXTREME STAGE LEFT ON THE FOYER.)**

                    VICTORIA:
                    I'm Victoria King. I'm trapped inside this lift. Please let me
                    out.

Expending her energy makes her feel dizzy.

Security Guard 1 comes running.

                    SECURITY GUARD 1:
                    (shouting) I hear you. Don't worry. We'll have you out
                    when we fix the controls.

Victoria, close to passing out.

                    VICTORIA:
                    I'm…dying in here.

Security Guard 1 produces a phone.

                    SECURITY GUARD 1:
                    Mr. Brayne, sir. Victoria King is trapped in the lift. (pause)
                    How long? Just let's get her out.

He opens the control pad by the lift and has a look.

                    BRAYNE:
                    (filtered) Don't touch anything. Someone will be round in
                    ten minutes.

                    SECURITY GUARD 1:
                    Did you hear that? Can you manage ten minutes?

Victoria at the air vent with the heel of her shoe again. It creates very
temporary relief of noise cessation and increased room temperature for ten
seconds.

                    VICTORIA:
                    I've been trapped in here since Friday afternoon. I don't
                    suppose ten more minutes will kill me.

As the noise starts up again Victoria slumps, as if robbed of all energy, to the
floor.

VICTORIA:
So long as it is ten.

Victoria passes out.

CURTAIN RISES EXTREME LEFT:

INT. PARENTS' HOME.
Phone rings. Patrick enters, yawning, in dressing gown. He picks the phone up.

BRAYNE:
We've located your daughter. She's been stuck in the lift at Thames Tower all weekend.

PATRICK:
What?!

Door opens and Elizabeth enters, tying her dressing gown too.

PATRICK:
Why didn't we think of that?

BRAYNE:
Someone will be here very soon. Of course, we'll all be there for the grand unveiling at nine.

PATRICK:
You think Victoria will want to go ahead with it the state she'll be in? (before he can reply) That's a rhetorical question by the way.

BRAYNE:
I'm sure she will. Victoria can turn even this round for maximum publicity.

PATRICK:
(outraged) I daresay she can garner publicity, but I don't think anyone can turn round the cost-cutting exercise you've been encouraging her on.

BRAYNE:
So I'm the bogeyman now. It'll all down to me.

PATRICK:
No. (pause before) I'm sure your particular kind of ruthless expertise is a great asset to Victoria professionally. But I'd back off personally if I were you. I know just how many women you've got in your little red book.

Brayne drops the line. Elizabeth turns to Patrick, who hangs up with a smile.

PATRICK:
Now we must tell Walter.

CURTAIN FALLS.

INT. LIFT SHAFT, THAMES TOWER.

RESCUE WORKER gets to the lift with his tools. Phone to hand.

RESCUE WORKER:
Tell her I'm in the lift shaft and I can see what's caused the blockage. As it was going up, the down mechanism failed to execute/stuck. It will take me half an hour.

INT. CORRIDOR OUTSIDE LIFT, THAMES TOWER.

SECURITY GUARD 1:
Half an hour? She won't make it.

Victoria moans in misery from within the **LIFT**, as if she's heard it.

RESCUE WORKER:
She will. Because I'll be blowing air down to her meantime.

He produces an air cylinder, directs it down the lift we see and releases the nozzle.

SECURITY GUARD 1:
Did you hear that, Victoria? The rescue man is already at work. And while he frees the lift mechanism, you'll start to feel more air coming in.

The air conditioning noise remains stubbornly. Victoria out for the count.

As the air continues, Rescue Worker takes his time to methodically unblock the lift mechanism. But it's trial and error.

Air starts to interrupt the monotone of the blocked vent.

As it breaks the sound once and for all, spreading inside the lift, Victoria stirs and perks up.

Rescue Worker makes final checks.

>RESCUE WORKER:
>Now.

In the **CORRIDOR STAGE LEFT**, Security Guard 1 presses the lift control.

LIFT doors open.

Security Guard 1 steps inside to see Victoria's faltering eyes light up. He rushes to embrace her and she him.

>VICTORIA:
>I've never been so glad to see anyone before.
>(singing at half strength)
>
>VERSE:
>*It won't be long now*
>*I can sense he's coming*
>*I hear his footsteps*
>*To take me from this confined numbing*
>*Here he is*
>*No matter who*
>*I shall be eternally grateful*
>*To live my life anew*
>
>CHORUS:
>*And I dream of falling in The Arms Of My Rescuer*
>*Sinking into his embrace*
>*Falling into The Arms Of My Rescuer*
>*Feeling myself touch base*

In The Arms Of My Rescuer
Looking up to see his face
Arms Of My Rescuer
Is where I finally get to interface

CURTAINS CLOSE:

BRIEF INTERVAL:

CURTAINS RISE:

8. INT. FOYER, THAMES TOWER. DAY.

LORD MAYOR arrives at the same time as Elizabeth, Patrick & a guilt-stricken Walter.

The **LIFT** before him opens. A dazed but cheerful Victoria appears with Security Guard 1 present.

> VICTORIA:
> This one. (nodding to Walter)

Victoria slumps into a disbelieving Walter's arms (he even looks around for the other feller), but she now sings "THE ARMS OF MY RESCUER" at full strength.

> VICTORIA:
> (VERSE) *They're at the door now*
> *Picking the lock*
> *Clinking clanking*
> *Now a knock-knock*
> *Here he is*
> *No matter who*
> *I shall be eternally grateful*
> *To live my life anew*
>
> CHORUS:
> *And I dream of falling in The Arms Of My Rescuer*
> *Sinking into his embrace*

Victoria does just that.

> VICTORIA:
> *Falling into The Arms Of My Rescuer*

Feeling myself touch base
In The Arms Of My Rescuer
Looking up to see his face

Victoria looks up to Walter.

> VICTORIA:
> *The Arms Of My Rescuer*
> *Is where I finally get to interface…*

Walter grabs her chin and as he makes to kiss Victoria passionately, her lips rush to meet his.

> VICTORIA:
> Walter. You were so right. If only I'd taken that detour in the park.

Walter close to tears, remembers: Fights to hold them back.

> WALTER:
> Sorry. Sorry. I know you don't like your men to be.. (cut off)

> PATRICK:
> (cutting in) I know one thing about my daughter.

> ELISABETH:
> Which is?

> PATRICK:
> She doesn't want men like Brayne who are double-dealing her, personally and professionally.

Victoria turns round, with an enquiring look.

> VICTORIA:
> I'd forgotten all about Brayne.

> ELISABETH:
> Very wise.

> PATRICK:
> Brayne's working as an inside man for your biggest rival.

He'll be prepared to jump ship in a year's time with what he knows.

VICTORIA:
Better he be pushed first.

Elizabeth consoles Victoria.

ELIZABETH:
Victoria, darling. We cannot begin to imagine what it must have been like in there.

WALTER:
There must have been times when you thought you'd never see the light of day again.

Victoria is rueful and turns to Walter.

VICTORIA:
And why did you forget I was in the Tower?

WALTER:
After Friday, I switched my phone off and went to ground.

ELIZABETH:
That's all forgotten now. We must cancel the Lord Mayor.

VICTORIA:
Cancel. No. Wait. This is an opportunity in disguise.
(raising voice)

The MEDIA – reporters, photographers, cameramen – gather. She courts them.

VICTORIA:
This was a disaster of my own making. I was the architect as well as the property developer of it. And I'm gonna use the unveiling to tell the world of my mistakes.

She points upwards.

VICTORIA:
And so I never forget, I want that lift in my office!

She leads the way **STAGE LEFT TO:**

9. EXT. FOYER, THAMES TOWER.

Lord Mayor cuts the tape. Also present is Helena, Steve & Mr. Flores.
Spotlight on Victoria. Reporter offers her a mike.

>VICTORIA:
>Although this is a day of celebration for Thames Tower and
>the people of London, my disappearance was at my own
>hands. To put it bluntly, if I hadn't underinvested with
>infrastructure that lift would not have jammed on me.

Gasps from the Media. Helena walks away, Steve closes his eyes, while Mr.
Flores gives her the thumbs-up. Elisabeth is comforted by Patrick.

>VICTORIA:
>If I hadn't tried to make savings, 24/7 staff would have been
>evident from as early as Friday afternoon, rather than the last
>minute before opening. My time in captivity has made me
>realise: success should not be tarnished with profit. We owe
>it to ourselves to do the very best we can. Lest we fall from
>grace or receive, in my case, a bitter lesson. I hope one day I
>deserve the title of Top Property Developer of the Year?

>VICTORIA:
>(sings "ONE THING AT A TIME").

>By the 2nd chorus, Walter, Elisabeth, Patrick and the Town
>Mayor have joined in.

>At the end of it, Insp Whiting appears on the scene, tape
>recorder to hand.

>INSP WHITING:
>(singing) *Ms Victoria King? I have a few questions for you.*

>VICTORIA:
>It's time for a few answers.

Surveying the Media reporters before her, Victoria selects one to ask a question.

REPORTER:
(holds mike out) Are you saying Thames Tower is currently unsafe?

VICTORIA:
All other checks and balances have been met. But we shall be looking at the building treatments again.

REPORTER 2:
Does that extend to other buildings in your property portfolio?

VICTORIA:
It does. And we shall no longer contest the subsidence case.

VICTORIA:
(singing "STUCK IN A LIFT FOR 3 DAYS")
(VERSE) *I never want to see the inside of a lift again*
Not in my lifetime I swear

No more confining four walls and clasping metal
More than I can bear
Yet bear it I have and come out the other side
It was a test of resilience bar none
I'll never forget a single moment
From the second it all begun

CHORUS:
I've Been...
Stuck In A Lift For Three Days
Wishing any other place I could be
I've Been
Stuck In A Lift For Three Days
And I'm glad as can be to be free
Stuck In A Lift For Three Days
Don't try it yourself, I implore
Stuck In A Lift For Three Days
From now the stairs I adore

VERSE:
My foot's over the threshold and joined by the other
Thank Goodness it's over at last

No more claustrophobia and assorted ills
I've worked through my demons full blast
And here I'am walking away from the lift
Never to enter again
Please take me back to civilisation

Away to where hopelessness wanes

Insp Whiting watches as everybody else joins in.

> INSP WHITING:
> (singing) *We've all got accounts to give.*
>
> VICTORIA:
> (smiles through gritted teeth) We're giving it.
>
> (singing)
> (CHORUS) *I've Been...*
> *Stuck In A Lift For Three Days*
> *Wishing any other place I could be*
>
> *I've Been*
> *Stuck In A Lift For Three Days*
> *And I'm glad as can be to be free*
> *Stuck In A Lift For Three Days*
> *Don't try it yourself, I implore*
> *Stuck In A Lift For Three Days*
> *From now the stairs I adore*
>
> REPEAT CHORUS

Victoria steps back, with Walter. Sensing she's moving away, Insp Whiting makes to intercept her.

> VICTORIA:
> I'm too tired to give you a full and proper account now. I've had an ordeal.

Insp Whiting reluctantly switches the tape recorder off.

As PEOPLE make to enter Thames Tower, Elizabeth and Patrick step back as Victoria and Walter step out towards the park.

CURTAIN FALLS STAGE LEFT INCLUDING THE LIFT:

CURTAIN RISES STAGE RIGHT:

9. EXT. PARK. DAY.

As Victoria and Walter walk through, the **ENTIRE STAGE** is taken up with the treeland walkway. Sun shines. Thames Tower seen in the distance.

> VICTORIA/WALTER:
> (sing DETOUR IN THE PARK with different outcome)

Victoria flings her arms round Walter.

> VICTORIA:
> Walter. I will marry you.

Walter hugs and kisses Victoria back.

> WALTER:
> Then so will I.

As they embrace, Walter handing Victoria an engagement ring, they sing "STUCK IN A LIFT FOR 3 DAYS".

ENCORE.

CURTAIN DOWN.

"STUCK IN A LIFT FOR 3 DAYS: THE MUSICAL"
Script & Lyrics
By ROBIN CALVERT © (2017)

ABOUT THE AUTHOR

www.robincalvert.co.uk

The BBC published one of Robin's monologues on the 5Live & Writersroom websites for WORLD CUP TAPES in 2006.

Robin graduated from the University of Central Lancashire in Preston with a first-class Bachelor Arts Degree in Film/Television Screenwriting (2011).

DR. WHO: MANY HAPPY SOLAR RETURNS covers the 1960s period, while DR. WHO: SOLAR RETURNS VOL 3 the early 70s.

The escapist spy-fi thrillers CLOAK AND DAGGER: OPENING GAMBIT (2012), CLOAK AND DAGGER: PANDORA'S BOX (2013), CLOAK AND DAGGER: EYE OF THE BEHOLDER (2014) & CLOAK & DAGGER: GUNS, TYRES, PURSUERS OF THE CHASE (2016) are published on Amazon.

GHOST STORIES UK VOL 3: MRS. HAMBLETON'S OTTOMAN (2014), Audio Download from www.wordofmouthproductions.co.uk

Robin has made a number of his screenplays - ABATTOIR, SUMMER BREEZE, CHRONOVISION & MANCRUISE - available and welcomes approaches from new film makers.

38817915R00042

Printed in Great Britain
by Amazon